"MONASTIC PREACHING IN THE AGE OF CHAUCER"

Siegfried Wenzel

"MONASTIC PREACHING
IN THE AGE OF CHAUCER"

Siegfried Wenzel

*The Morton W. Bloomfield Lectures
on Medieval English Literature, III*

MEDIEVAL INSTITUTE PUBLICATIONS

WESTERN MICHIGAN UNIVERSITY

Kalamazoo, Michigan

1993

This publicaton is made possible by the Morton W. Bloomfield Lecture Fund, supported in his memory by contributions from his family, friends, colleagues, and students.

The Bloomfield Lecture
I. (1989) George Kane
II. (1991) Jill Mann
III. (1993) Siegfried Wenzel

Printed in the United States of America.

ISBN 1-879288-39-7

MONASTIC PREACHING
IN THE AGE OF CHAUCER

As the Middle Ages drew to an end—in England, the late fourteenth and fifteenth centuries—, the great monastic orders certainly cannot be said to have vibrated any longer with an energetic intellectual and spiritual life. The age of saintly founders
and reformers of orders and of houses that not only fostered the
spiritual life but also led to the highest achievements in the
liturgy, architecture, learning, literature, and the making of
manuscripts, had long since gone. What in earlier centuries had
been achieved by Benedictine and Cistercian monks was now
paralleled or even superseded by the hearts, heads, and mouths
of members of newer orders, primarily Dominican and Franciscan friars. Such decline and sterility seems to characterize the
monks' activity as preachers as well. In consequence, preaching
by members of the older monastic orders and before monastic
audiences during the last medieval centuries has never attracted
much interest among historians or literary scholars. To be sure,
the large-scale overviews of medieval preaching in general—
Schneyer's for Germany, Longère's for France, and Owst's for
England,[1] give us the names of some monk preachers who were
active in the fourteenth and fifteenth centuries. But at the same
time, these historical accounts draw a picture in which monks
had occupied the stage during earlier ages, their preaching
attaining a climax with Saint Bernard of Clairvaux in the twelfth
century, but from about 1200 on yielded the task of preaching

1

the Good News to the new orders, the friars, whose work from then on dominates our modern attention. The reason for the historical shift from monks to friars is not hard to see: by definition, monks withdrew from the world and lived lives that were devoted to the performance of the liturgy and to the pursuit of an ideal of holiness that was to be attained within the walls of the cloister; on the other hand, the new orders that came into being shortly after 1200 made it their business to go out and preach God's word to the masses—St. Dominic and his fellow preachers to heretics and wavering Christians in southern France, St. Francis and his companions to the masses in the Italian countryside as well as the newly flourishing urban centers, who were then not being reached by the established parish clergy or the older religious orders. Hence it is that in the view of modern accounts, once Dominicans and Franciscans began their tremendously energetic work of preaching, the older monastic orders nearly lose all significance in the history of preaching during the later medieval centuries. In Gerald Owst's words:

> By the time ... that the age of Fitzralph and of Wycliffe has begun, all the great names in the history of monastic eloquence have disappeared, and the pulpit here seems to share in the general decline of cloister fame and cloister influence ... Vital, potent interest in preaching ... appears to be dead. This fact may possibly be reflected in the actual dearth of fresh monastic sermon literature for the periods under our examination.[2]

While there may be some truth to the general tenor of this assertion, its details are by no means accurate and call for revision, because the later fourteenth century witnessed a definite resurgence of interest in preaching among Benedictines and other monastic orders, and fresh monastic sermon literature produced near the end of the fourteenth and the early fifteenth centuries does in fact exist. The renewed interest in preaching left its traces at various levels, from monastic legislation to actual sermon collections. In 1336, Pope Benedict XII, himself a devout Benedictine monk, issued a bull that revitalized earlier monastic customs and formulated precise laws about two aspects of Benedictine life in England that were closely related to preaching: the provincial chapter and higher studies of monks at the university, to which I shall return in a moment.[3] Signs of this renewed interest can likewise be found in relevant activities of individual monks that are known to us by name. For example, John Sheppey of Rochester priory (c. 1300–1360) left two manuscripts filled with sermons given by preachers including Franciscans which he collected while he was studying at Oxford.[4] Another monk, Thomas Brunton from Norwich, collected the sermons he had preached while he was bishop of Rochester between 1373 and 1389.[5] Rochester priory itself owned a copy of the great collection of preaching materials made by the Dominican John Bromyard, which is so well known to and frequently quoted by students of Chaucer and Langland.[6] And still another monk, Ranulph Higden from Chester (died 1363 or 1365), even wrote a handbook for preachers.[7]

There are, in addition, monastic records that tell us of particular occasions at which monastic sermons were given. The most detailed information we have concerns the provincial chapter. The already mentioned bull by Pope Benedict XII, *Summi magistri*, ordered that the heads of Benedictine houses in both ecclesiastical provinces of England, that is, Canterbury and York, should no longer meet separately as they had done for some time, but come together in one place every three years to discuss and legislate on matters pertaining to the order in England. That was indeed done, from 1338 on, in the geographical center of England, Northampton. A good number of records have preserved detailed accounts of the agendas of these chapters as well as the ceremonies that accompanied them. Thus, as the chapter opened, all the abbots and priors and other clergy who had traveled to Northampton would, at the sign of a bell, assemble to hear a mass of the Holy Spirit. When mass was over, the bell would ring again, and the attendants then proceeded to the chapter house, where they put on their monastic habits and listened to a sermon, which was preached in Latin, "as it was fitting." When that was over, all secular clergy had to leave, and the business of the Benedictine provincial chapter began in earnest. Two days later, the chapter would close with another procession, mass, and sermon, but this one was to be given "to the people in the vulgar tongue," that is, presumably, in English. Just before these closing ceremonies, the chapter had already selected preachers who were to give these two sermons at the next provincial chapter three years later.[8] Our records have preserved the names of several preachers who were assigned to these occasions as well as the biblical texts for their sermons and occasionally even the amount of whatever remuneration they received for their labors.[9]

Similar formalities were used for chapter meetings in individual houses, especially when the community gathered for such momentous events as the election of a new abbot[10] or, in the case of Canterbury, the archbishop.[11] Some preaching may also have occurred at the daily or weekly chapter meetings in each Benedictine monastery, at which matters concerning the welfare of the community and the morals of its individual members were discussed, though such preaching has left no unequivocal traces in the manuscripts I have drawn on. Another occasion at which a sermon was given before the monastic community was the visitation, when a member of the same or a different order or any high-ranking prelate came from outside to see if all was well within a monastic house.[12] Thus, in 1378, the large monastery of St Albans was visited by two monks from Ramsey, one of whom started the check-up with a sermon.[13] Again, some forty years later, the same monastery was visited by the prior of Bardeney, who preached a sermon on the thema "A wellspring rose from the earth." It is pleasant to hear that "in this visitation they found nothing except that all things were worthy of praise."[14] Among several surviving visitation sermons, one explicitly states that preaching on this occasion was indeed "customary in our order."[15]

And there were other special occasions thus distinguished with a sermon, ranging from the profession of two monks at St. Albans in 1430[16] to the funeral ceremonies for Duchess Blanche of Lancaster, whose sermon, delivered by the bishop of Cloyne,

4

Ireland, has, as far as I know, to the regret of Chaucerians not been preserved.[17]

But Benedictines gave sermons outside the monastery as well. In the beginning years of the fifteenth century, several monks from Canterbury are on record as having preached at various synodal meetings in London, an honor they shared with the bishop of Carlisle as well as the Franciscan provincial for England.[18] Yet another occasion must not only be mentioned but highlighted, because of the relatively large number of extant sermons connected with it. This is the preaching of academic sermons at the university, presumably Oxford. By the end of the fourteenth century, Oxford had three study houses for Benedictine monks: one only recently founded by and for monks from Canterbury; another for monks from Durham priory, which by then was about a century old; and the third—Gloucester College on the grounds of what today is Worcester College—for students that came mostly from southern England and equally in operation for about a century. These foundations owed their existence to various orders coming all the way from Rome. Though Pope Benedict and his predecessors did not actually found a college, dreading, as it were, to leave an illiterate ministry to the Church they were certainly much concerned with educating the clergy including young monks. A number of mandates thus stipulated that each Benedictine house was to send a determined proportion of its younger members to the university, where they should live in a common house of studies, and that their abbots were to make sufficient funds available so that these young men could devote themselves to the study of theology and, to a lesser degree, canon and civil law (1336).[19] Such papal orders were not only eagerly taken up by the English provincial chapter but in fact extended. In particular, the bull *Summi magistri* had only spoken of theology and law as disciplines for which monks should be sent to the university.[20] In the resolutions issued by provincial chapters in England, however, we find an added, strong emphasis on preaching as another subject to study at the university. For example, the chapter of 1338 declares:

In order that our faith, which through the ages has spread its fronds from sea to sea, may be fittingly illumined by the bright rays of virtues, it has been firmly enjoined through the aforementioned presidents [of the chapter] by apostolic authority that each prelate is to ordain and instal those from his convent whom he knows to be able and prepared for the office of preaching, to preach God's word both in private and in public, with wisdom and discretion, so that the candle that has once been lighted may not be hid under the bushel but, placed on a candlestick, may shine forth to all who are in the house of God.[21]

And a later chapter, probably of 1363, makes it clear that some monks were sent to Oxford, not to read philosophy or theology but specifically to learn how to preach. The prelates meeting at this chapter, after recommending that students of philosophy and theology should engage in regular disputations, then turned their attention to "those who are sent to the university for the single purpose of learning how they may fittingly preach God's word to others," and ordered that they,

according to the disposition made by their prior and the more advanced students preach frequently both in Latin and in English, in our common study house in Oxford or elsewhere, as their prior and the more advanced students may decree. In this way they will be able to preach more boldly and readily when it is necessary to recall them to their monastery.[22]

And indeed, other records tell us not only of students returning to their monasteries for major feast days and preaching there to their spiritual family,[23] but also of established Benedictine university professors being recalled to look after the business of preaching at home.[24]

In this wide array of occasions for preaching, one place and time one would have expected to find, however, is missing, and that is the normal parish church on a Sunday morning. The reason for this absence is that Benedictine monks were normally not in charge of parishes and did not engage in the cure of souls. Although many monasteries held parish churches as their property and sources of income, the required pastoral duties were usually carried out by non-monastic vicars appointed for that purpose.[25] On the other hand, we must remember that many of those magnificent buildings which make the Middle Ages so delightfully visible to present-day visitors to England: Westminster Abbey, Canterbury Cathedral, the cathedrals at York, Worcester, Winchester, Durham, Rochester, and many others, were formerly parts of monastic institutions. These are large churches which must have been filled with layfolk for the Sunday and other services. It stands to reason that in them monks not only said mass and heard confession but also preached on occasion. Quite recently Dr. Joan Greatrex has studied the extant documentary evidence from Worcester and pointed out that in 1290 the pope granted the monks there licence "to preach in public before the people in Worcester and in other churches belonging to them or of their patronage." A number of unpublished records from the fourteenth and early fifteenth century further indicate that indeed Worcester monks were charged with preaching in public, were payed for it, and were called home from Oxford for just that purpose.[26] Similarly, Thomas Brunton was asked to come home from Oxford to preach in the monastic cathedral of Norwich;[27] and after he became bishop of Rochester, he preached not only in his own cathedral in the city but at several churches in the coutryside as well.[28]

The records on which I have so far relied, therefore, show quite clearly that in the fourteenth and fifteenth centuries Benedictines were actively interested in the office of preaching and in fact practiced it on a variety of occasions. This much has been known for some time. What has remained obscure to date is precisely what was said on those occasions, and in what form it was spoken; in other words, what has been missing in this picture are actual sermons made and preached by English Benedictines. The sermons by bishop Thomas Brunton, which were edited nearly forty years ago, are not as helpful in this respect as one could hope, since they were given to all sorts of audiences and hence can, in their totality, not be considered characteristic of a specifically monastic milieu. In contrast, my own work on bilingual sermons from the age of Chaucer has led me to a number of precisely such sermons, which have so far not received the attention they deserve as documents of monastic preaching. I must stress that this material has come to my notice coincidentally, in the wake of trawling the seas of manuscripts in search of macaronic pieces of whatever provenance. Undoubtedly there are other manuscripts in existence that contain further fruits of Benedictine preaching in the period from about 1380 to about 1430; but I am confident that the material I will in the following draw on gives us a good and sufficiently trustworthy picture of what English Benedictines spoke from the pulpit during this period.

But first a few words must be said about how we know that a given sermon is monastic. Medieval manuscripts, alas, never contain neat title pages that might say something like, "Monastic Sermons by Dom So-and-So, published at St. Mary's Abbey, York, in 1399." Even worse, manuscripts of sermons more often than not gather a wide variety of pieces that were given before all sorts of audiences, monastic and otherwise, and were very probably not written by a single author. Thus, the best we can do is to examine each sermon separately, look for incidental notes in the margins, and often be content with inferences drawn from the texts themselves. The surest kind of evidence for monastic provenance would be a title or a marginal remark that tells us the name of a monk who wrote or preached the piece. Thus we learn that John Paunteley gave a sermon at the funeral of Walter Frouceter, abbot of Gloucester, on May 3, 1412;[29] or that Master John Fordham, who is known to us from other sources as a monk from Worcester priory, preached a sermon at the general chapter;[30] or that Hugh Legat, a monk from St. Albans, made a sermon for Passion Sunday.[31] Somewhat less satisfactory are rubrics that tell us that a sermon was preached in a definitely monastic environment but that withhold the name of its preacher. For instance, we hear that one piece was delivered "at Northampton in the general chapter of the black monks," and another similarly "in convocation or the general chapter."[32] But even such brief marginal labels are, unfortunately, extremely rare, and the search for monastic sermons must often be satisfied with clues that occur within the texts of the sermons themselves. Here our best indication comes from direct references to the order and its founder. Such remarks as "our venerable father Benedict"[33] or "the lawgiver of monks, the most holy father Benedict"[34] or "we religious who entered the religious life and strive to be imitators of blessed Benedict"[35] or "let us not be followers of Epicurus but ... rather imitate, as per our rule, the footsteps of our patron, who in fact and name was Benedictus"[36] clearly establish the religious affiliation of the preacher and his audience. Yet another possible indicator is the form of address used at the beginning of a sermon. Sermons beginning with "Reverendi domini" or "Venerandi patres et domini" indicate that their audiences were clerical, though these need not have been monastic communities. To be sure of the latter, one must look for further support from the text itself, support that may include certain stylistic features that also occur in undoubtedly monastic pieces. For example, the already mentioned Master John Fordham of Worcester cultivated a style and rhetoric of his own, and even used a peculiar form of address in the sermon which bears his name. When we find the same features elsewhere, we can reasonably add further pieces to his output.

With the use of these various indicators one can establish a fairly sizeable and certain corpus of Benedictine sermons made and preached in the period with which I am concerned. In the following, I will limit myself to those sermons that address a Benedictine audience explicitly. There are, in the manuscripts I have examined, about thirty-five that do so clearly.[37] Four of them were given at provincial chapters, four or five at visitations, and two to a university audience, most likely at Oxford. In addition, beyond one funeral sermon we have six or seven pieces for various Sundays or feast days of the church year, and at least a dozen for saints feasts. The latter are for Saint Alban, Saint Benedict, and the Blessed Virgin, who received a surprising total of seven sermons.

As one might expect, sermons in honor of a saint are basically eulogistic oratory, and indeed much in this entire body of

9

texts follows the conventions of medieval pulpit rhetoric in both form and content. Like medieval preaching in general, monastic sermons largely exhort their audiences to do penance and strive for the good life by praising virtues and condemning vices. Rather than belaboring these commonplaces, I will focus on three more particular concerns that strike me as characteristic and significant. These relate to the monastic ideal, the state of the nation, and the intellectual life.

The monastic ideal is, in our sermons, not unexpectedly presented as having a special and privileged status in God's kingdom on earth:

> The heavenly husbandman—order and measure of the entire sub-lunary world as well as the eternal mansion … planted a chosen vineyard in a rich soil, namely our holy monastic order … The plants of this monastic vineyard have given such strength to the garden of the church on earth that before all other orders it grows strong in its vines, blossoms in its sprigs, and constantly brings forth fruit in its grapes; it gets often tied fast with the bonds of obedience, cleaned out with diligence through giving up one's property, dug up deeply through mortification of one's flesh, and enlarged through health-giving statutes and counsels.[38]

Thus the monastic life is said to have been established as a special school, a *gymnasium* superior to the Platonic Academy in Athens, because in it divine Wisdom herself has made her dwelling place to teach man virtue and to help him on his way to heaven.[39] Its founder in the West, Saint Benedict, was a second Abraham because he left his kin and homeland to follow God's call and promises and was rewarded with a large offspring.[40] His disciples have vowed themselves to walk the narrow path; they are set to worship the divine name before all other men, and their lifestyle is exemplary for the whole church. Monks must be models to all Christians by the holiness of their life and their works of contemplation. "You who are more firm and experienced in Christian spiritual warfare," says one preacher, "must feed your brethren, namely by teaching and example … , now in devout prayer, now in waking, now in chastising your bodies by fasting, and in practicing other works of a similar nature."[41]

The cornerstones of this lifestyle and the foundation of monastic discipline are the traditional vows of obedience, poverty, chastity, and stability of place. In a life shaped by the rule of St Benedict, these vows translate into such specific practices as submitting oneself to the will and guidance of one's superior, fasting and praying, abstaining from meat, guarding one's senses, and keeping silence. If this rule is truly observed, it will foster humility, charity, and love, and lead to the peace of a community that lives in complete harmony.

> Let us therefore give our hearts to God through silence and holy meditation with respect to our intellect; through love and compassion with respect to our will; and through obedience, chastity and the renunciation of our possessions with regard to our actions, so that clad in this threefold armor of our monastic life, by following the footsteps of our father Benedict we may keep ourselves the more securely unstained of the world.[42]

The harmonious community thus aimed for, so Master John Ford tells the abbots and priors gathered at the provincial chapter, is like a living organism. It must not be "a tumultuous crowd but a group of people at peace forming one mystical body" in which "the minds of all individuals should be bound to each other inseparably with the bond of charity and the glue of love, so that, like members in one and the same body, they suffer or rejoice with each other over" whatever bad or good fortune might befall a single member of their community.[43] In this living organism, different members have different functions. The majority of monks would devote themselves to prayer and contemplation, while a few others would serve as officers of the monastery and look after the necessary physical, economic, and financial details to ensure the conditions for a life of contemplation. Finally the abbot or prior would rule and guide the whole house with wisdom, strength, and clemency.[44] It is interesting to note that in this analysis of different functions within the same organism, the active life of monastic officers is often discussed in almost apologetic tones: they are absolutely necessary to the fulfillment of the religious vocation of all the monks and must not be looked down upon as, so to speak, second-class citizens. In the words of another sermon, which uses a simpler twofold pattern,

> the city of our religious life is, as it were, governed and protected by two kinds of troops. Our officials and administrators of temporal goods procure and provide what is necessary for the life of the brothers and defend the rights of our order against the outside. At the same time, our cloistered monks give themselves to continuous prayer, to meditations on scripture, and to the performance of the divine services. Thus Mary is at her leisure and Martha is busily at work.[45]

But sermons by nature deal not only with ideals and virtues, they also look at vices and failings. Hence a number of those directed to Benedictine audiences speak, however generally, of the moral shortcomings and the decadence which the entire order has fallen into. Things nowadays are no longer what they once were. "Where under the roof of the cloister, I pray," one preacher exclaims, "do we find a Jerome who through his prolonged zeal for virtue and his diligent reading tries to come to the light of true learning and a knowledge of letters? Nor can hardly anyone be found who with Bernard savors the sweetness of devotion," and so forth.[46] Not only do the main goals of the monastic life remain unattained, but the very activities and practices typical of cloistered life as it is regulated by Saint Benedict's Rule are being neglected:

> To our monks of today the sweetness of holy reading does not appeal, the eagerness of devout prayer has faded, and devotion to contemplative holiness has become tedious. Where, I ask, does the ready obedience of our holy fathers still rule? Where are that perfect charity and genuine humility that once flourished in the cloistered school for an honest life, that is, the paradise of monks? If I must speak the truth, obedience is dead, humility is banished, charity has vanished away, and that honorable reverence that

12

younger monks ought to give to the advanced years of their seniors has, through boyish levity, been turned into derision. Now the limits of modesty are being overstepped, the discipline of fasting is broken, and the tongues of quiet monks who should attend to holy readings and keep a devout silence, are loosened for frivolous and idle tales in the treasury of the cloister. And so they often seem to practice the school of virtues, not in exercises of pious contemplation, but rather in strife and contention.[47]

Such behavior of course goes directly against the foundation of the monastic life, the Rule:

Our rule suggests and commands that at opportune times we observe silence; but certain monks go directly against this when they take no care to guard against scurrilous words and foul speech in the choir or the dormitory. Our rule commands us to observe a religious and disciplined lifestyle; but some monks go directly against this when they take too much delight in fanciful, precious, and superfluous clothing. Our rule tells us what is sufficient for our livelihood and admonishes us to be modest and sparing in what we eat and drink; but some monks go directly against this when they think they may eat as often and whenever and in whatever places they desire and engage in drunken revelry and singing until midnight. Our rule forbids us to leave the cloister without permission from the abbot or prior; but some monks go directly against this when, contrary to canon law, they go hunting in fields and woods with loud shouting and keep hunting dogs in the monastic enclosure ... We monks are held to celebrate Mass twice or three times a week; but some monks go directly against this constitution when they claim they are unfit or indisposed to celebrate because of their administrative duties ... And when such monks are reproved for their abuses in chapter, they try to defend their sins against their superiors, to appeal the penalties they receive according to the rule, and to murmur and rebel against the commands and counsels of their superiors.[48]

To these infractions of monastic regulations and practices I will add two further failings that might be of special interest for historians of literature. First, the vice of slander and envy, which not only reappears in several laments of this kind but is frequently singled out for more detailed elaboration:

> If a monk studies or devotes his time to contemplation, they call him a hypocrite; if he practices patience, they call him timid; if he strives after simpleness, they call him a fool; if he is intent upon justice, they call him impatient; if he is devout, they call him an oddball; if he is solicitous about his preaching, they say he is after praise; and if he is well liked by the people, they call him a flatterer.[49]

So it is no wonder when, in contrast, a funeral sermon eulogizes the deceased abbot of Gloucester at some length for

> this commendable quality, that he would not willingly hear any evil about anyone, nor believe any stories, and if he heard any, he would interpret them in the best way ... It was extremely difficult to make him think ill of a friend. And even if someone told him something bad about his friend, he would answer as Socrates did with regard to his disciple: "So you say," as if he were saying, you have said so, whether it is true or not.[50]

The other peculiar feature is the lament at the decadence in monastic book production:

> In former times both older and younger brothers used to write books with their own hands. Many wrote a large number of codices in the free time they could snatch between the canonical hours of prayer, and they devoted times that were set aside for their bodily rest to the making of books. As a result of their labors, sacred treasuries shine in many monastic houses to our day, filled with divers books, to give salutary knowledge to those who wish to study it and a pleasant light on their way to others ... But alas, books are yielding to Bacchus, compilation gives way to compotation,

and so on.[51]

Complaints at current vices, at the falling off from a higher state that had been reached in the past, also form part of the

14

second major concern that appears throughout these monastic sermons, namely the lamentable condition of contemporary society. It is especially a group of very remarkable pieces in manuscript Bodley 649 that return again and again to this topic, sermons that have deservedly drawn the attention of such church historians as Professor Roy Haines.[52] Using several different images, such as the ship of state or the vineyard, the preacher speaks of the glory and high reputation England enjoyed in the past, both at home and abroad. "All Christian nations," he says in once case,

> once feared and honored the English because of their strength, their good government, and the good life they led. While our ship was thus steered with the rudder of virtue, we traveled on a sea of wealth and prosperity. Fortune was our friend, our honor increased. But as soon as virtue declined and vices began to rule, Fortune changed her face and our honor started to wane. Our ship was so feeble, our enemies set so little store by us, that the little fishing boats of Wales were about to oversail us. Through pride and sin we traveled from wealth to woe. There was much woe and tribulation in this country; many mishaps rose up among us on account of sin; storms of conflict and dissent blew up hard. Our ship was so hurled and tossed about among tempests and straits that is was in great peril and often in danger of drowning.

He then lists a number of specific political upheavals that occurred in the reigns of Richard II and Henry IV, but eventually goes on to praise Henry V, "this wise mariner, this most worthy warrior," for leading the ship of state out of those troubled waters into the new glory achieved at Agincourt.[53]

The same group of sermons links another theme to that of military decadence, namely the coming of heresy, which has undermined faith and traditional religious practices. It is the Lollards, normally referred to by that name, who have sown tares in the English wheat and who are leading simple folks astray with their erroneous teachings about the Eucharist, the spiritual power of pope and parish priests, the effectiveness and required use of the sacraments, and the legitimacy of giving tithes and of following such traditional practices as praying to saints, worshipping images, and going on pilgrimages.

This anti-Lollard stance and the pride in England's military achievement are very characteristic of the sermons in MS Bodley 649; but they appear also elsewhere in Benedictine preaching. In one of the Middle English sermons contained in a manuscript of Worcester Cathedral and edited by Grisdale, for example, the preacher, after mentioning the Lollards by name, exclaims:

> You see well what battles and war we have among us, may God for his great mercy stop them in good time! What pestilence also, what scarcity of goods, for there is hardly anyone, whether poor or rich, who does not complain about his goods. Yea, and many other countries look at us with hatred and scorn and hold us to be the worst people, the most false under the sun. And this, trust you well, is because of our wickedness and our bad morals and these cursed errors and heresies that are upheld in our midst.[54]

I now turn to the third major concern of Benedictine preaching, the intellectual life. A number of sermons express without equivocation the view that learning is an integral and necessary part of the monastic existence. We have already heard one preacher lament that manuscripts are no longer copied, and another look in vain for the likes of Saint Jerome and his great learning. The ideal is nicely formulated in a sermon that likens the monastery to a vineyard and concludes that, like the lily which is pale in its roots, green in its leaves, and redolent, monks should "grow pale in the fruitful recitation of holy scripture, ... put forth green leaves in writing books, and ... spread a sweet odor in acquiring knowledge."[55]

Such learning included the technical study of philosophy and theology as it was undertaken at the university. One of the monastic sermon collections I am dealing with has preserved several formal eulogies of these disciplines in what must have been opening lectures in academic courses on Peter Lombard and the Bible. These pieces link graduate study at the university intimately to the monastic and contemplative life. And they expect that monk students bring a greater seriousness and holier life to the university than their fellow students:

> The more we progress in learning, the more we are obligated to grow in good morals and increase in virtues, and to display this increase publicly. For the monk student must appear more mature in his behavior than others, less given to laughter, more pure in his speech, more humble in his bearing, more meek in appearance, more devout in his dress, so that whoever looks at him will grant that he sees a son of Saint Benedict, an angel of the Lord as it were, indeed the very rule of life.[56]

Concern with the intellectual life shows itself further quite concretely in the style of these sermons. Their general structure is unvaryingly that of the so-called scholastic sermon, with its peculiar logical and rhetorical rigor that underlies their tight logical and verbal structure and a careful, often labored development. These sermons are not products of the moment, of an ad-hoc inspiration, but instead smell of the lamp and midnight oil. They are learned, in the sense of gathering a wealth of carefully chosen and apt biblical and other quotations, and they are sophisticated, often to the point of being tortuous, in carrying out the structural rules set forth in contemporary arts of preaching. The result must often have been appealing to refined intellects, though one suspects that it also may have left some hearts rather cold and, perhaps, some faces blank and yawning. There is a little vignette of some relevance in a contemporary monastic chronicle which I cannot help finding rather amusing in this respect. In 1374 King Edward III called together a council at Westminster. There the king and the archbishop of Canterbury sit in the middle, with the higher prelates of the realm next to the archbishop, and the lords of the kingdom next to the king. In front of them are four masters of theology on a bench: the provincial of the Franciscans, the Benedictine monk Uhtred from Durham priory, the Franciscan friar John Mardesley, and an Austin friar. The pope had written to king Edward claiming that he, the pope, was the general overlord over all temporal possessions of the church in England, and Edward now wants to know what his higher churchmen think of that. So the archbishop says, yes, we can't deny that the pope has such overlordship. The Franciscan provincial begs to be excused until he has recited the hymn "Veni Creator Spiritus" or at least said a Mass of the Holy Spirit. Then our monk gets up and

> answers in the form of a sermon, taking as his beginning the verse "Lo, here are two swords," by which he intends to show that Peter has both temporal and spiritual lordship.

But when he sits down, Friar Mardesley rises to his feet, quotes the scriptural words "Put your sword into its sheath," and shows that those swords do not signify temporal power.

> Which he did by quoting Scripture and the gospels, with authoritative words of the fathers as well as the example of monks who left their possessions behind, and with decretals from Canon Law.

The discussion goes on for quite a bit longer, in which the archbishop mumbles, "We had good advice in England without the friars," and in turn gets himself called "ass" by his king.[57] But what matters in this little drama for our purposes is the apparent difference in the style in which Benedictine monk and Franciscan friar—both incidentally university men and professors—address the issue and clash: one producing a sermon on a text that was an old chestnut in discussions of this issue, the other evidently furnishing a more rational argumentation based on a much wider array of texts and proofs. Friar Mardesley simply throws the book, not only at the papist position but also at Dom Uhtred of Boldon.

I should, in all fairness, add that the British historian William Pantin has called this account "a picturesque but probably unreliable passage," possibly "fictitious and in the nature of a pamphlet."[58] But whatever its historical accuracy may be, the impression of stodginess, rhetorical inefficiency, and even political irrelevance which the account conveys of Master Uhtred is of course precisely what lies at the root of the modern view of the decline of monastic preaching with which I began this lecture. And yet, I have to say that this impression does not do justice to the reflections of an intellectual and literary life that I find in the monastic preaching of around 1400. For one thing, these sermons quote, not only the Bible, church fathers, and pagan writers, as any good medieval sermon does, but also medieval poets of more recent vintage. Especially Alanus of Lille appears in several Benedictine sermons, with quotations from both his *Anticlaudianus* and the *De planctu Naturae*.[59] Another medieval poem, likewise of the twelfth century, that finds its way into monastic preaching is the *Architrenius* by John of Hanville.[60] In addition, these sermons show a knowledge of classical literature which, by medieval standards, must be called respectable. This appears not only in the fact that monastic preachers borrowed stories from Ovid which here come from farther afield than the normal run-of-the-mill material, but also in the very style these Benedictine writers cultivate. They do not hesitate to refer to the Almighty as *rector Olimpi*[61] or speak of Homer's Golden Chain.[62] Nor do they refrain from weaving classical allusions intimately into monastic discourse, as in the following sentence, where the allusion to the labyrinth of the Minotaur appears suddenly without a previous reference to the classical myth:

> You therefore, reverend brethren, ... with the thread of our reasonable Rule as your guide walk out of the labyrinth of such abuses.[63]

Nor do they abstain from producing some scintillating rhetorical firework, often at points where, of all places, they protest their own humility:

> If I had acquired the keys of worldly knowledge with Paul and had learned all kinds of languages so that I could, with the honey-sweet voice of Mercury, pass beyond the flowery verbal eloquence of Cicero's throat, I would still be found to be insufficient, dumb and ignorant when it comes to speak the praise of our keeper [the Blessed Virgin].[64]

19

The speaker of these lines identifies himself as a junior member of his community, and one could therefore see in the quoted lines the rhetorical exuberance of an undergraduate fresh home from, say, Oxford or Harvard. Yet more mature heads took an equal delight in starting a sermon off with similar fireworks or addressing the assembled heads of religious houses as *patres conscripti*, as if they were Roman senators,[65] and putting in an ironic aside that some of them might have come to the provincial chapter in order to taste what he labels "Falernian cups" rather than attend to the order's business.[66]

This is rather different from the revival of interest in classical myth and fable which engaged earlier fourteenth-century friars and which Beryl Smalley has called attention to.[67] Like those friars, monastic preachers also draw on Ovid and moralize with gusto, but as my quotations will have shown, their classical learning penetrates more deeply into the very texture of their style than is the case with the preaching friars. Such affinity with the classics was by no means a new phenomenon in the fourteenth century; it can also be found in monastic authors of the twelfth century, where it has received some fine attention in Father Jean Leclercq's study of monastic culture.[68] The point here is that the sermons I have been discussing show that around 1400, English Benedictines were keenly interested in cultivating intellectual pursuits, which included reading the classics and using this knowledge in their preaching, an interest that appears not only in the sermons I have been examining but also more generally in the large collections of classical material made, for instance, by Thomas of Walsingham and John Whethamstede, who were both Oxford-trained monks living in the monastery of St. Albans.[69]

During the years in which I had the privilege of sharing Morton Bloomfield's intellectual presence and receiving his scholarly guidance, he himself was immersed in a study of medieval monasticism and its possible influence on *Piers Plowman*. This lecture is not the occasion to evaluate the book that resulted from those studies. But it is an entirely appropriate and accurate tribute to the man and his wide-ranging learning which these lectures commemorate if I conclude by stressing that, beyond the evidence Morton had at his disposition a generation ago, the material I have here surveyed certainly bears out his hunch that in the 1370's and 80's English Benedictine monasticism was anything but a dead institution and spent intellectual effort.

Notes

1. Johannes Baptist Schneyer, *Geschichte der katholischen Predigt* (Freiburg i. Br., 1969); Jean Longère, *La prédication médiévale* (Paris, 1983); G. R. Owst, *Preaching in Medieval England. An Introduction to Sermon MSS of the Period c. 1350–1450* (Cambridge, 1926; repr. New York, 1965).

2. Owst, *Preaching*, p. 49.

3. See David Knowles, *The Religious Orders in England*. Vol. 2: *The End of the Middle Ages* (Cambridge, 1955), pp. 3 ff. The bull, *Summi magistri*, has been printed in Wilkins, *Concilia Magnae Britanniae et Hiberniae* (London, 1737), 2:588 ff.

4. These are MSS Oxford, Merton College 248 and New College 92; see G. Mifsud, "John Sheppey, Bishop of Rochester, as Preacher and Collector of Sermons," unpublished B. Litt. thesis, Oxford, 1953. A more recent account of Sheppey is given by Alberic Stacpoole, "Jean Sheppey," in *Dictionnaire de spiritualité ascétique et mystique*, vol. 8 (Paris, 1974), pp. 763–64.

5. *The Sermons of Thomas Brinton, Bishop of Rochester (1373–1389)*, ed. Sister Mary Aquinas Devlin, 2 vols., Camden Third Series, 85–86 (London, 1954).

6. Now British Library, MS Royal 7.E.iv (*Summa predicantium*).

7. See Margaret Jennings, ed., *The Ars Componendi Sermones of Ranulph Higden O.S.B.* (Leiden, 1991).

8. This brief account is based on the statutes issued by the provincial chapter of 1343; see W. A. Pantin, *Documents Illustrating the Activities of the General and Provincial Chapters of the English Black Monks 1215–1540*, 3 vols. (= *Chapters*), Camden Third Series, 45, 47, 54 (London, 1931–1937), 2:58–61. Some of the practices described are also recorded for earlier chapters, both before and after the two provinces were united in 1336.

9. See for example Pantin, *Chapters*, 2:12, 13, 15, 19–20, 26, 97, 155, 156, etc. The statutes of 1444 stipulate a fee of 40 shillings (2:216–17).

10. At St. Albans, 1326; see Thomas Walsingham, *Gesta Abbatum Monasterii Sancti Albani*, ed. Henry Thomas Riley, Rolls Series 28, part 4, vol. 2 (London, 1867), p. 183. Again, in 1396: part 4, vol. 3, p. 426.

11. Roy Martin Haines, *Ecclesia anglicana: Studies in the English Church of the Later Middle Ages* (Toronto, 1989), pp. 17, 27, 32.

12. Owst, *Preaching*, pp. 52–4.

13. Walsingham, *Chronicon Angliae*, ed. E. M. Thompson, Rolls Series 64 (London, 1874), p. 203.

14. *Chronicon rerum gestarum in monasterio Sancti Albani*, in Rolls Series 28, vol. 3, pt. 5.1, p. 38.

15. "Cum iuxta laudabilem ordinis nostri consuetudinem visitacionem precedere sermo debeat salutaris," Sermon W-113, f. 220v. For the format by which I refer to sermons see below, note 37. All translations of Latin, Middle English, or macaronic texts in this paper are my own.

16. *Chronicon rerum gestarum in monasterio Sancti Albani*, p. 53.

17. *Gesta abbatum*, Rolls Series 28, vol. 4, pt. 3, p. 277.

18. Wilkins, *Concilia*, 3:273.

19. Knowles, *Religious Orders*, 2:14–24.

20. Chaps. 7–8 regulate study of "sciencie primitive" (grammar, logic, and philosophy) and higher studies (theology and the two laws), but do not mention preaching; Wilkins, *Concilia*, 2:594–6.

21. Pantin, *Chapters*, 2:11–12.

22. Pantin, *Chapters*, 2:76.

23. Pearce, *Monks of Westminster*, p. 27. In 1384, archbishop Courtenay had to order that monk students do not stay at home for more than 2 weeks: W. A. Pantin, *Canterbury College*, 3 vols., OHS, n.s., 6–8 (1947–1950), 3:176.

24. Knowles, *Religious Orders*, 2:58.

25. Margaret Jennings has discussed the subject of monks and the cure of souls, without adducing much evidence: "Monks and the *artes praedicandi* in the Time of Ranulph Higden," *Revue Benedictine* 86 (1975), 119–28.

26. Joan Greatrex, "Benedictine Monk Scholars as Teachers and Preachers in the Later Middle Ages: Evidence from Worcester Cathedral Priory," in Joan Loades (ed.), *Monastic Studies* II (1991), 213–25.

27. Knowles, *Religious Orders*, 2:58.

28. See the headnotes to his sermons in the edition by Devlin.

29. R-03, edited by Patrick J. Horner, F.S.C.: "John Paunteley's Sermon at the Funeral of Walter Froucester, Abbot of Gloucester (1412)," *ABR* 28 (1977), 147–166.

30. W-069.

31. W-002; edited by D. M. Grisdale, *Three Middle English Sermons from the Worcester Chapter Manuscript F.10* (Leeds, 1939), pp. 1–21.

32. British Library, MS Titus C.ix, f. 26; and W-028, edited by W. A. Pantin, "A Sermon for a General Chapter," *Downside Review* 51 (1933), 291–308.

33. "Venerabilis pater noster Benedictus," Cambridge, MS Jesus College 13, art. vi, f. 67v.

34. "Monachorum legislator, sanctissimus pater Benedictus," R-05, f. 29v.

35. "Nos religiosi, qui religionem ingressi sumus et beati Benedicti imitatores esse contendimus," R-18, f. 88.

36. "Non simus igitur discipuli Epicuri sed ... regulariter imitantes vestigia nostri patroni re et nomine Benedicti," R-29, f. 143v.

37. They are, with their occasions: O-06 (3 Lent?); O-24 (Assumption, preached to Franciscans?); O-25; R-03 (funeral); R-06 (general chapter of Cistercians); R-18 (visitation); R-29 (Christmas Eve); R-31 (St. Alban); W-004 (Assumption; also in R-05); W-005 (Christmas Eve); W-013 (4 Lent; in English, to lay people?); W-028 (general chapter); W-069 (general chapter); W-098 (to clergy); W-100 (Conception or Nativity of Blessed Virgin Mary); W-101 (Deposition of St. Benedict); W-109 (St. Benedict); W-113 (visitation); W-114 (visitation?); W-115 (St. Benedict); W-117; W-120 (Assumption); W-123; W-124; W-126 (visitation?); W-127? (St. Benedict); W-129 (Good Friday); W-130 (university); W-131; W-134? (Vigil of Assumption); W-135 (Assumption); W-139? (to clergy); W-148

(Maundy Thursday?); W-149; W-151 (Good Friday); W-152 (Assumption?); W-162 (university); Cambridge, Jesus College 13, art. vi, ff. 67v-70 (St. Benedict); British Library, MS Titus C.ix, ff. 26–27 (general chapter). The sigla used here refer to: O = Oxford, MS Bodley 649; R = Oxford, MS Laud misc; 706; and W = Worcester Cathedral, MS F.10. Detailed inventories and discussions of O, R, and W can be found in my forthcoming study of macaronic sermons.

38. "Celestis quidem agricola, metrum et mensura tocius ordinis sublunaris et etheree mansionis, a luce prima in vesperam sue fabrice influens incrementa, vineam quandam electam in loco vberi, sanctam scilicet religionem monasticam, in vitibus sanctorum patrum nostrorum primo in Egipti partibus plantatam ad horam quam postea ab inimici lupi rapacitate sua dextera adquisitam in tocius Christianissimi [sic] terminos transtulit et transduxit. Cuius vinee monastice plantule terram orti militantis ecclesie sic firmarunt quod pre ceteris aliis religionibus in vitibus viret, in palmitibus floret, in botris fructificat incessanter, ligatur frequencius per funes obediencie, purgatur diligencius per abdicacionem proprietatis, foditur profundius per mortificacionem carnis proprie, et propagatur per salutaria statuta et consilia," W-126, f. 147ra.

39. W-069, f. 130rb.

40. In W-028, Abraham is considered the founder of monasticism: "Iste ergo princeps Abraham gerens tipum aptissimum prelatorum exemplare, monachatus posuit fundamentum," Pantin, "A Sermon," p. 298. Other references to Abraham in W-109, f. 217; W-131, f. 256vb.

41. "Qui estis solidiores et experti in militia religionis Christi, fratres vestros pascere, suple doctrina et exemplo, ... nunc videlicet deuote orando, nunc vigiliis insistendo, nunc corpus ieiuniis castigando, ac ceteris consimilibus bonis operibus semper inherendo," W-134, f. 261v.

42. "Sic ergo corda nostra Deo demus per silencium et sanctam meditacionem quantum ad intellectum, per amorem et compassionem quantum ad effectum [read affectum], per obedienciam, castitatem, et proprietatis abdicacionem quantum ad effectum, ut hac triplici armatura nostre religionis armati qua nostre professionis executores effecti imitando vestigia sanctissimi patris nostri Benedicti ab hoc seculo ... nosmetipsos securius," Cambridge, Jesus College MS 13, art. vi, f. 68v.

43. "Vt igitur hec congregacio religiosa et religio congregata non tumultuosa turba sed multitudo pacata et vnum corpus misticum veraciter censeatur, sic insolubiliter caritatis compage et glucio dileccionis

adinuicem colligandi sunt animi singulorum, vt ad instar diuersorum membrorum in eodem corpore que iuxta variam fortune exigenciam sibi inuicem compaciuntur eciam et congaudent quidquid vni acciderit quadam amica vicissitudine et vnione gratissima ad cumulum doloris vel gaudii omnes reputent esse suum," W-069, f. 130vb.

44. W-126 analyzes these three groups of monks and their functions in the "vineyard" of the monastery at some length.

45. "Due quasi milicie sunt quibus regitur et protegitur ciuitas nostre religionis. Nam sicut officiales ministratores temporalium procurando et prouidendo fratribus vite necessaria et iura ordinis extrinseca defendendo mercione militant in acie sua, sic claustrales continuis oracionibus insistendo et in scripturis meditando ac eciam diuinis vacando seruiciis valde militant eciam in acie sua, sicque dum Maria vacat ocio, Martha ministrat," W-152, f. 294x.

46. "Sub claustri namque tecto, vbi iam queso reperitur Ieronimus qui per frequens virtutis studium leccionisque diligenciam ad vere sciencie lumen et litterarum noticiam nititur peruenire? Iam vix habetur aliquis qui cum Bernardo tante deuocionis sapit dulcedinem ut eterni solis splendorem, Christum Dei Filium, per interne meditacionis morulam sine graui fastidio valeat intueri," R-29, f. 142v.

47. "Modernis namque claustralibus sacre leccionis non sapit suauitas, deuote oracionis languescit sedulitas, ac contemplatiue sanctitatis deuocio iam redditur tediosa. Vbi queso sanctorum patrum obediencia regnat sine mora? Vbi caritas perfecta seu humilitas non simulata, que quondam in uirtuoso honeste conuersacionis studio claustrali, scilicet paradiso floruerant monachorum? Certe, si verum fatear, obediencia iam moritur, humilitas proscribitur, et caritas euanescit, honorisque reuerencia que maturis seniorum etatibus foret a iuuenibus exhibenda iuuenili leuitate sepius uertitur in derisum. Iam metas modestie excedit sobrietas, sacri ieiunii violatur integritas, ac mutorum lingue claustralium qui sacris leccionibus uacantes assidue deuota seruarent silencia, circa friuolas vanitatis fabulas in claustri sacrario reserantur. Sicque scolam virtutum non ad pia contemplacionis exercicia sed ad contencionis litigia videntur frequencius exercere," W-004, f. 16v.

48. "Nobis enim suadet regula nostra ac precipit oportunis temporibus silencium obseruare, et obstat quorundam monachorum abusio, qui nec in choro nec in dormitorio nec in claustro curant verba scurilia et turpiloquia precauere. Precipit nobis regula nostra religiose et ordinate incedere, et obstat quorundam monachorum abusio qui in vestibus

curiosi[s] operimentorum preciositate et superfluitate non modicum delectantur. Prestat nobis regula nostra victus sufficienciam et suadet in cibis et potibus modestie parcitatem; cui obstat quorundam monachorum abusio qui estimant sibi licere quocienscumque et quandocumque et quibuscumque locis indifferenter commedere et vsque ad mediam noctem suis potacionibus et aliis cantacionibus inhonestis insistere et vacare. Precipit nobis regula nostra claustrum sine abbatis aut presidentis alcius [?] non exire; cui obstat quorundam monachorum abusio qui contra canonicas sancciones presumunt in agris et siluis venacionibus clamosa voce intendere et infra ceptra monasterii canes venaticos retinere. Preterea, secundum scilicet Constitucionem Benedicti pape XII capitulo 27, tenemur nos monachos bis vel ter celebrare singulis septimanis; cui obstat quorundam monachorum abusio cuiusmodi sunt obedienciarii, qui dicunt se propter suas administraciones minus ydoneos et indispositos ad celebrandum. ... Tales, karissimi, monachi si pro predictis abusionibus in suis capitulis pro[...]tur, statim contra precidentes sua peccata nituntur defendere, correcciones regulares appellare, et contra superiorum precepta et consilia murmurare et pertinaciter rebellare," W-124, f. 241vb.

49. "Si quis studeat vel contemplacioni vacet, dicunt enim quod ypocrita est; si paciencie, timidus; si simplicitati, fatuus est; se iusticie, impaciens est; si religioni, singularis est; si predicacioni ... , appetitor laudis; si coram hominibus acceptus fuerit, adulator est," W-120, f. 234vb.

50. "Sed inter cetera habuit commendabilem condicionem: noluit libenter audire malum de aliqua persona, noluit credere fabulis, etsi audiret aliquam, vellet construere in partem meliorem. Et hoc fuit causa sue quietis et aliorum. Et si quisquam sibi suum reuelaret consilium, nusquam vellet detegere. Foret eciam valde difficile alicui facere ipsum male opinari de amico suo. Et siquis referret sibi malum de suo amico, responderet quandoque ad instar Socratis pro suo discipulo, 'Tu dixisti,' quasi diceret: cum verum vel non, tu ita dixisti," R-03, f. 19. The sermon has been edited by Horner, *ABR* 28 (1977), 147–166.

51. "Olym namque claustrales senes cum iunioribus vineas et vites librorum propriis manibus conscripserunt. Scribebant nonulli codices plures inter horas canonicas interuallis captatis, et tempora pro quiete corpori commendata fabricandis codicibus concesserunt. De quorum laboribus vsque in hodiernum diem in plerisque splendent monasteriis aliqua sacra gazophilacia diuersis libris plena ad dandam scienciam

salutis studere volentibus atque lumen delectabilem semitis aliorum. ... Sed prothdolor ... iam fertur Liber Bachus respicitur et in ventrem ...itur, liber codex despicitur et a manu eicitur, sicque calicibus epotandis non codicibus emendandis indulget hodie studium plurimorum," W-126, ff. 247vb-248ra. In translating the last sentence, where complaint leads to verbal punning, I have employed some poetic license in order to reproduce in English the kind of wordplay that a modern audience is familiar with from the rhetoric of Jessie Jackson. The pun *codices/calices* appears again in W-135, f. 263v.

52. Most recently: Roy M. Haines, *Ecclesia anglicana. Studies in the English Church of the Later Middle Ages* (Toronto, 1989), pp. 201–21 and 333–50; earlier publications are listed on p. 333, n. 2.

53. O-25, edited by Roy M. Haines, "'Our Master Mariner, Our Sovereign Lord': A Contemporary Preacher's View of King Henry V," *MS* 38 (1976), 85–96. The quoted passage appears on pp. 89–90.

54. W-013, edited by Grisdale, *Three Middle English Sermons.* The quoted passage appears on pp. 41–2.

55. "Lilia enim pallent in radicibus, candent in foliis, virent in foliis, et redolent in humoribus atque granis. Sic enim claustrales psallerent [*sic; read* pallerent] in fructuosa sacre scripture recitacione, virerent in librorum composicione, et redolerent in sciencie adquisicione," W-125, f. 248ra.

56. "Quantum in doctrina proficimus, tantum in morum honestate siue augmento virtutum succrescere et in huius incrementi protestaciones et signa ostendere obligamur. Debet namque scolasticus monachus ceteris in gestu apparere maturior, in risu suspensior, in affatu honestior, humilior in incessu, mansuecior in aspectu, religiosior in ornatu; vt quicumque talem attenderit, quasi filium sanctissimi Benedicti, quasi angelum Domini, tanquam ipsam normam viuendi se inuenisse concedat," W-130, f. 256rb.

57. See the account in Knowles, *Religious Orders,* 2:66, and in M. E. Marcett, *Uhtred de Boldon, Friar William Jordam and Piers Plowman* (New York, 1938), pp. 16–18. The event is reported in *Eulogium historiarum,* ed. Frank Scott Haydon, Rolls Series 9 (1863), vol. 3, pp. 337–9.

58. W. A. Pantin, *The English Church in the Fourteenth Century* (Cambridge, 1955; American edition, Notre Dame, 1963), p. 167.

59. Especially in R-31, f. 154, and perhaps in W-014, W-103, W-139, and Cambridge, Jesus College MS 13, art. vi, f. 78v.

60. R-31, f. 154v.

61. W-139, f. 269.

62. W-149, f. 288vb, and W-162, f. 333v.

63. "Vos igitur, reuerendi mei, quos iurate religionis votiua constringit professio habitusque autenticat in conuersacione monasticus, filo regulate racionis conductore harum abusionum conclusio uelocius discedite laborinto dulcedine litterarum vberius recreati," R-31, f. 155v.

64. "Reuera si claues sciencie seculi suscepissem cum Paulo, omniumque genera linguarum hactenus taliter didicissem vt cum Mercurio mellite vocis dulcedine floridam uerborum eloquenciam Tulliani gutturis superarem, circa nostre procuratricis laudem non solum insufficiens reperirer, verum inscius et ignorans, mutus pariter et elinguis omnibus apparem," W-004, f. 16v.

65. "Patres conscripti" appears in W-069, f. 130va, and W-162, f. 333.

66. British Library, MS Titus C.ix, f. 26v.

67. Beryl Smalley, *English Friars and Antiquity in the Early Fourteenth Century* (Oxford, 1960).

68. Jean Leclercq, *The Love of Learning and the Desire for God: A Study of Monastic Culture*, trans. Catharine Misrahi (New York, 1961), chapter VII. A more specific study of such classicizing style is R. W. Southern, "Peter of Blois: A Twelfth-Century Humanist?" in *Medieval Humanism* (New York, 1970).

69. See Antonia Gransden, *Historical Writing in England. II. C. 1370 to the Early Sixteenth Century* (Ithaca, NY, 1982), chapters 5 and 12.